104

Highly Successful School Principals

EMPOWERING LEADERS TOWARDS EXCELLENCE

DR. PRIYANKA MEHTA

INDIA · SINGAPORE · MALAYSIA

Notion Press

No.8, 3rd Cross Street
CIT Colony, Mylapore
Chennai, Tamil Nadu – 600004

First Published by Notion Press 2021
Copyright © Dr. Priyanka Mehta 2021
All Rights Reserved.

ISBN 978-1-64850-630-7

PREFACE

The world called 'school' is a campus like no other place of work. It is not just a place; it is a vision. The dynamics are far too challenging. The role and responsibility of being the head of a school have evolved and continues to change.

As Principals, we all face situations that test our skills and question our abilities to make the best decisions. We all wish to answer the question in affirmative when it comes to how good we are in our capacity to lead a school.

The quality of being an 'ideal' school Principal targets means and mechanisms of dealing with people, satisfying stakeholders and making an impression among students across a spectrum, much beyond the boundaries of the campus.

104 Traits of Highly Efficient School Principals is a review for all school leaders to explore the power of effective school management. The ideas shared are tried and tested, over two decades of teaching and learning, analyzed at various platforms, aimed at effective school management while delivering goals of education.

We look forward to your precious feedback via mail.

Hoping for a happy transformation!

Educationally yours,
Dr Priyanka Mehta

ACKNOWLEDGEMENTS

I am excited to share my thoughts and experiences in the form of a book for my fellow educationists. I am thankful to all my friends, colleagues and well-wishers for encouraging me and sharing their good wishes and ideas, thus making this book a possibility.

This book was motivated by my parents, my daughter, Manasi, who has been my constant critic, and my better half, Binoy, who has been inspiring and supportive of me and my work.

Gratitude to Dheeraj Mehrotra for being a great friend and mentor, for always reinforcing the confidence in me to venture into this new domain.

I sincerely hope that the following pages guide you in your journey towards becoming a better-than-before Head of School.

Happy learning as you read!
– Dr Priyanka Mehta

UNDERSTANDING THE BOOK

"The greatest discovery of my generation is that human beings can alter their lives by altering their attitudes of mind."

– William James

The book defines 104 refined traits of being a leader at school. Each quality is more than just a statement. It's a practice for mind and actions, something that can help you analyze a situation in a perspective that we know but may not recall or are not sure to believe in.

Each trait can help you understand and relate with a situation in a way that is better, such that the reaction or action to follow is carefully gauged and calibrated. Some of these may act together or separately or one at a time.

A very careful comparison has been drawn of the leader within you to the 'strategic leader' defined by the famous Chanakya, through his famous verses. The idea is to help you position yourself, in thought and action, to lead the school effectively.

Whatever you do, remember, the attitude is most important and that it can only be optimistic. Focus on the 'can' rather than the 'cannot' and on possibilities rather than the limitations. Your attitude is the foundation, it all starts and ends with it!

Most of the time, we fume and fret over the people we deal with. What we have is actually not of importance. What makes a huge difference is what we can do with the people at our disposal. Even the last pawn on the chessboard is essential!

Each trait here takes you closer to becoming the best...

"Rulership can be successfully carried out (only) with the help of associates. One wheel alone does not turn.

Therefore, he should appoint ministers and listen to their opinions."

– Arthashastra

#1
TRAIT

An efficient Principal is a human first then a leader.

- Practice purpose with understanding— 'We' more than the 'I'.

- Empathy is a great virtue. However, learn to draw a line.

#2
TRAIT

An efficient Principal knows when to lead from the front and when to lead from behind.

- ➤ Different times require different and distinct approaches.

#3
TRAIT

An efficient Principal spends time and energy in designing the school.

- Each and every corner of the school reflects your intention.

- Spend extra time to make the staff rooms warm and cosy.

- That's where your vision takes shape!

#4
TRAIT

An efficient Principal is honest with him/her-self and with the team and must set examples before others as a benchmark to be emulated in the future.

#5
TRAIT

An efficient Principal knows his/her shoes and wears them smart and comfortable, both at work and parties!

- This is a quality benchmark for all stakeholders!

#6
TRAIT

An efficient Principal always makes a positive point—both in the real and the virtual world.

- You get known for your 'online reputation' and for actions on the campus.

- 'Social distancing' is a good trait at times.

#7
TRAIT

An efficient Principal believes in 'first impression' and 'intuition'.

- Believes in quality of thought, action and outcome.

- Remember, you are creating a lasting impression on those you know and many beyond.

#8
TRAIT

An efficient Principal is compassionate, with a clear understanding of not being overdriven by the feeling.

– Do the balancing act.

– Let the 'head' and the 'heart' play equals.

#9
TRAIT

An efficient Principal is approachable.
He/she does not rule from the ivory tower.

- Avoid monologues.

- Step in and become a part of the action.

- Actions always speak better than words.

#10
TRAIT

An efficient Principal is just!

- He/she gives equal opportunities to all at work, priority being the fulfillment of goals and objectives—both organizational and individual.

"If situated between two stronger kings, he (the ruler) should seek shelter with one capable of protecting him."

– Arthashastra

#11
TRAIT

An efficient Principal is firm but polite.

- Believes in 'Yes', ' It can be done', the first time and every time.

- Works with complete knowledge of flaws, displaying a high level of commitment.

#12
TRAIT

An efficient Principal is connected to the outer world as much with the inner.

— It's all about being resourceful and being connected and up to date.

#13
TRAIT

An efficient Principal values work, character and people.

— He/she puts ethics and values above all

#14
TRAIT

An efficient Principal works. Be in the team while you lead the team.

– Don't be a preacher, you are not in school to deliver sermons.

#15
TRAIT

An efficient Principal defines clear goals.

- He/she helps set 'smart' goals for all.

- It is important to know the capacity of the team, individually and together.

- Set realistic goals, keeping the last in performance in mind.

- Be an enabler.

#16
TRAIT

An efficient Principal plans with the team, and for the team.

— A possibility towards 'together everyone achieves more'.

#17
TRAIT

An efficient Principal is a teacher first and a learner for life.

- Must have things to do 'more' in the bucket list all the time.

#18
TRAIT

An efficient Principal says 'sorry' easily.

- Must accept the responsibility of anything that may go wrong.

- At the same time, avoid taking all the credit.

- Remember to praise your team when the situation demands.

#19
TRAIT

An efficient Principal wears a 'smile' no matter how ruffled the feathers may be.

— She/he must shadow perfection.

#20
TRAIT

An efficient Principal connects with children as a priority.

— Must learn from them and interact with them all the time.

For the first five years love your child, for the next ten years discipline them, and after that, consider them your friends .

— Arthashastra

#21
TRAIT

An efficient Principal easily partners with parents, builds trust and dependability.

➥ It matters! They have a lot at stake.

#22
TRAIT

An efficient Principal must read and encourage reading as a trait in the team too.

- Deliver the learning during assemblies and classroom interactions.

- Inspire to turn learning into action.

#23
TRAIT

An efficient Principal is a good listener.

- Don't try to prove others wrong all the time or talk too much about yourself.

- Listening to others helps in gauging them, thus helping you to predict their thoughts and actions.

- Observe while you listen.

#24
TRAIT

An efficient Principal is a person of no anger.

- Give it up!

- Be a person of few words, especially when you are angry or upset.

- It is natural, but learn to let it go.

- Release yourself and your mind, work light!

#25
TRAIT

An efficient Principal must be a great storyteller. The Pied Piper and the Disney, all in one!

→ Let your creative exuberance shine.

#26
TRAIT

An efficient Principal must never judge people or be judgmental.

- Most of our impressions rise out of the experiences of the past.

- They are certainly not the right parameters to fairly judge anyone.

#27
TRAIT

An efficient Principal must never propagate 'Pyjama' rules.

- Rules and instructions should be specific to the organization and its people.

- The team must know why rules are there, and it's even better if these are made with them.

- Clarity in expectations aligned with resources available helps a team to perform better

#28
TRAIT

An efficient Principal always lives in the present with his/her focus on the future.

- If you continue to live in the past, it becomes your future.

- Learn from the past, don't dwell on it.

- Believe in the Law of Dominant Thought—what you focus on... expands!

#29
TRAIT

An efficient Principal shares and gives it all to the team.

- His/her experiences and knowledge are a resource for the team.

#30
TRAIT

An efficient Principal opens up to the team for feedback and ideas.

➤ More is always better than one.

➤ Each member of the team is capable of sharing at least one brilliant idea, thus leaving you powered with many to choose from.

A potential minister must have–
The desire to learn
Ability to listen effectively
Ability to reflect
Ability to reject false views
Intent on truth, not on the
person
.....And in all cases, he should
favour the stricken like a father

– Arthashastra

#31
TRAIT

An efficient Principal does not possess a tunnel vision.

- Do not be rule-bound.

- Be flexible and creative.

- Make the best and most out of your opportunities.

#32
TRAIT

An efficient Principal handholds and does the balancing act so that none in the team falls.

— Believe in team performance.

#33
TRAIT

An efficient Principal empowers, trains and creates more leaders.

- Remember, you are not going to be there forever.

- Empowering people elevates your excellence.

- Don't be insecure, always nurture and nurse talent.

#34
TRAIT

An efficient Principal analyzes his/her patterns.

- He/she analyzes situations at work or otherwise repeatedly, with the same or different people, but leading to the same results.

- These patterns come from your sense of belief and esteem, which contribute to the outcomes.

- Be aware of these, both the negative and the positive ones. Work on them and improve.

#35
TRAIT

An efficient Principal works on his/her-

- Intelligence Quotient (IQ),

- Emotional Quotient (EQ),

- Spiritual Quotient (SQ), and most importantly,

- Technology Quotient (TQ).

#36
TRAIT

An efficient Principal doesn't forget the real person he/she is.

- Nothing has to be sacrificed within you to be a new person.

- Be yourself!

#37
TRAIT

An efficient Principal leads the change and is not scared of it.

- Start with small steps and build your change muscles gradually.

- Plan the change so that your plan does not change!

#38
TRAIT

An efficient Principal must never be a 'Yes, Boss!' person.

- You have been hired to do the right thing in a better way.

- Voice your opinion politely, even if it does not match.

- There are chances that yours shall be appreciated.

#39
TRAIT

An efficient Principal knows when to say 'no' to both the superiors and juniors.

➤ Be on the right side of the fence and never be taken for granted.

#40
TRAIT

An efficient Principal has challenges ready for the team.

- ➤ He/ she does not let anyone go complacent.

- ➤ A busy team is a happy team.

Wealth is not only what is with you
But also what is 'in' you

– Arthashastra

#41
TRAIT

An efficient Principal works for vision and goals, not just for the sake of work and being hired to be there.

➤ Find the answer to 'what justifies your presence there', keep the need burning.

➤ Nobody is indispensable but get close to becoming one!

#42
TRAIT

An efficient Principal does not and must never work for charity.

- Free does not have value and can be easily set aside or ignored.

- Being on a mission is different!

#43
TRAIT

An efficient Principal maintains a daybook.

- Sounds ancient but works across ages.

- We are not superhumans to not forget.

- Missing out on things can be embarrassing at times while at others, it can lead to a delay in work.

- Reminders are an excellent idea.

#44
TRAIT

An efficient Principal is optimistic.

-- This is a feeling and a quality he/she passes on to the team as well.

-- Being optimistic is being a game changer!

#45
TRAIT

An efficient Principal should always find out how the subordinates feel after meeting him/her.

- This will help in understanding if one can handle teams well or not!

#46
TRAIT

An efficient Principal makes sure that the team knows its abilities and limits.

- They must know how high they can soar.

- Attempting to fly without wings is foolish, more if you are made for the water.

#47
TRAIT

An efficient Principal pays attention to details, especially situations at work.

- They don't happen by accident.

- They are the reflection of the system, its people, processes and beliefs.

- Work to elevate thinking and skills; it will create magic!

#48
TRAIT

An efficient Principal is visible, but not a watchman.

- Too much of a check is a deterrent to performance.

- Also, too much visibility induces dependability.

- An effective system is one that runs without you.

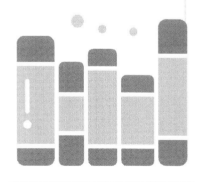

#49
TRAIT

An efficient Principal is a mentor to all.

- *Strong teams make you stronger.*

- *Alone, you only get exhausted.*

#50
TRAIT

An efficient Principal is not a joker, so please don't try to please all.

- That's not what you are there for.

- While aiming for the goals, you are bound to shake people out of their comfort zones.

He, the king, should strive to
impart training to the prince.

– Arthashastra

#51
TRAIT

An efficient Principal is friendly but not a friend to teachers.

→ Maintain that distance.

#52
TRAIT

An efficient Principal strikes a balance
with the management.

- Stakes of the management are too high.

- Staying at loggerheads 'always' is not
  advised.

#53
TRAIT

An efficient Principal knows that all battles are not yours to fight.

- Choose your battles—we know we need to fight odds at all steps.

- But always fighting and at wrong places can tire you.

- A tired leader is like a defeated one.

- Lack of strength diminishes creativity, most essential to a leader.

- More so, you are not amongst enemies.

- You deal with teams!

#54
TRAIT

An efficient Principal dreams and teaches the team to dream.

- From dreams comes the drive to achieve.

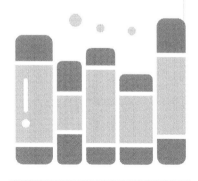

#55
TRAIT

An efficient Principal never keeps secrets from the core team.

- There is a difference in keeping secrets and sharing information not supposed to be shared on strategic grounds.

- Your core team should be developed and groomed to be trustworthy.

#56
TRAIT

An efficient Principal knows his/her strengths and weaknesses.

- Do not over exhibit or underestimate yourself.

#57
TRAIT

An efficient Principal must remember that every team has a formula, which works around Gardner's theories of multiple intelligences.

- To keep them engaged and motivated, have something for each one to do successfully.

#58
TRAIT

An efficient Principal is an expert at all dimensions of learning and pedagogies of facilitating learning in the classroom.

➥ Your school is your laboratory. Explore and experiment.

#59
TRAIT

An efficient Principal must know what each teacher teaches in her class.

— Ignorance can be dangerous and may also lead to low performing teams.

— Read lesson plans, call for notebooks, make test sheets and sometimes... teach!

#60
TRAIT

An efficient Principal always remembers Claxton's 4Rs.

- Resilience

- Resourcefulness

- Reflection

- Relationships

All undertakings should be
preceded by consultation.
Holding a consultation with
only one, he may not be able
to reach a decision in difficult
matters. With more councilors it
is difficult to reach decisions and
maintain secrecy.

– Arthashastra

#61
TRAIT

An efficient Principal is not necessarily a 'strict' or a 'loud' principal.

- Train your team so that they know where and when to draw a line.

- Shouting and creating noise does not prove a point.

- Unpleasant music makes you plug ears.

- You definitely do not want people turning deaf to your instructions.

#62
TRAIT

An efficient Principal is a tough taskmaster but a kind administrator.

➤ Be understanding but not predictable.

#63
TRAIT

An efficient Principal is a juggler.

- He/she must know how to multitask, and when you do, do not wait for people to acknowledge.

- It is not a circus; it's your job.

#64
TRAIT

An efficient Principal must be smart enough to manipulate for the good of the people and for the school.

- As an administrator, one must know when to bend to the gust of wind.

- Trees with hard trunk get uprooted during a storm, while the soft bushes bend and survive.

#65
TRAIT

An efficient Principal never cribs and cries in public.

- You are a leader, and leaders survive the odds.

- You must know when and where to speak and how much!

#66
TRAIT

An efficient Principal can gauge talent and skill carefully.

- Do not be emotional while choosing a team.

- Dead weights and low performers should not be given a second chance.

- You travel long when you travel light and with active teams.

#67
TRAIT

An efficient Principal is creative.

- Sometimes thinking less helps you to be more creative and make better decisions.

- Be patient and take time in saying a 'yes' or 'no' or 'nothing'.

#68
TRAIT

An efficient Principal is the one who never thinks he/she knows it all.

➥ You must remain hungry to know more forever and be a learner for life.

#69
TRAIT

An efficient Principal is a happy human being.

- Make sure this happiness is infectious and percolates down to the last man in the organization.

- Happy teams last longest!

#70
TRAIT

An efficient Principal makes sure he/she rests, relaxes and sleeps enough.

➤ Ensure to make time for family and, above all, for yourself!

*Wars are not fought in the
battlefields
But in the minds of the generals.*

– Arthashastra

#71
TRAIT

An efficient Principal always finishes work on time.

- *You must schedule your time well and maintain minimum delays.*

- *Stay-backs for yourself and for the team are a bad reflection on time and work management.*

#72
TRAIT

An efficient Principal is a problem solver.

- You gain the confidence of the team if you step in and give solutions to the issues rather than wasting time in scolding people and blame gaming.

- Understand that mistakes happen due to reasons of deficiency in people.

- There is no point in reiterating the same.

- Find a support system for them.

#73
TRAIT

An efficient Principal must have powers of persuasion.

- It is not enough to have a vision and a team.

- You should be able to sell your vision and make it a shared vision.

#74
TRAIT

An efficient Principal knows that more important than having a team is knowing what you can get done from them.

➤ Having goals to match the team increases the performance graph for all.

#75
TRAIT

An efficient Principal is a motivator and a good role model.

- Great leaders don't just sit in their offices and give orders.

- They demonstrate the actions and values that they expect from the team.

#76
TRAIT

An efficient Principal is a hands-on worker.

- He/she gets involved in daily work wherever and whenever needed.

- He/she stays in touch with what happens anywhere in the school—it's all your business!!

#77
TRAIT

An efficient Principal does not push timelines ahead.

— Even if it is done once, the team gets used to it. Remember, a habit is very difficult to change.

#78
TRAIT

An efficient Principal is a psychologist and a mind reader.

- Further, you should be able to read the body language of the person you face to make sure you respond appropriately.

- Don't forget to play the fortune reader too sometimes!

#79
TRAIT

An efficient Principal must know when to intervene and how.

- It is important to understand if we are going to plan a path for the subordinate and help him/her find one.

- Being authoritative or facilitative, depending upon the circumstances, is a crucial decision to take.

- We must know when to confront, support or prescribe.

#80
TRAIT

An efficient Principal is a
transformational leader.

- Given the resources, abilities and
  skills in the different stakeholders, the
  principal collaborates to achieve shared
  goals.

The excellences of the king are ...
intelligence and spirit

– Arthashastra

#81
TRAIT

An efficient Principal is a people's person with high communication skills.

- You cannot afford to be an introvert or imagine people to understand what you think on their own.

- Effective communication leads to effective leadership.

#82
TRAIT

An efficient Principal is a manager.

- → You manage everything—people, resources, processes, results, and so on.

#83
TRAIT

An efficient Principal looks for reasons to appreciate the team.

– Be generous in appreciating good work and choose your words well while you remark an underperformance.

An efficient Principal is not emotional him/her-self but manages to kindle the emotions of others.

→ Most of the time, difficult people come around if handled emotionally.

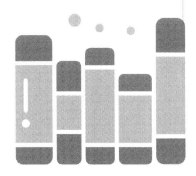

#85
TRAIT

An efficient Principal is a trainer who must know the developmental needs of the team members and help them meet their career goals.

— It is our duty, as mentors, to help them discover their potentials.

#86
TRAIT

An efficient Principal needs to be an economist and an accountant, manage resources within the budget and save too!

#87
TRAIT

An efficient Principal needs to set quality benchmarks for teachers and students on the go.

#88
TRAIT

An efficient Principal is a great visionary, looks for a possibility in every challenge.

— *Never misses an opportunity to serve the Mission and Vision of the school.*

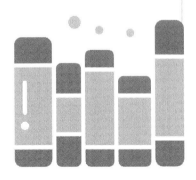

#89
TRAIT

An efficient Principal 'Walks' the talk.

➡ Not talks the talk or walks the talk!

#90
TRAIT

An efficient Principal believes in 'Learning to Learn' as a hobby instead of occasional occurrence concerning quality deliverables in the school system.

An arrow, discharged by an archer, may or may not kill one person, or may not kill even one; but the intellect operated by a wise man would kill even children in the womb

– Arthashastra

#91
TRAIT

An efficient Principal believes that 'Gaming' is important in real life to learn and explore the sportsmanship towards excellence in daily affairs.

- Learn to play with ideas and thoughts

- Keep the rules of the game in view when in fight

- A sports person is not for the field alone!

#92
TRAIT

An efficient Principal is not a 'shake the pan' person.

- Buy peace; don't stir your team too much.

- Keeping them ruffled induces restlessness and a lack of confidence in subordinates.

#93
TRAIT

An efficient Principal has to have the spirit of wisdom, with the ability to stay calm under pressure as one of the greatest assets of one's personality as a whole.

#94
TRAIT

An efficient Principal is never afraid to experiment.

- He/she is open to ideas, innovation and implementation towards excellence.

- Taking calculated risks towards the unknown makes you the 'First' among many!

#95
TRAIT

An efficient Principal delivers with passion, makes a strong first expression, and connects with the audience with pleasure and pride.

#96
TRAIT

An efficient Principal learns more by listening.

- Believes in working together and dwells wisdom from patient hearing from all stakeholders.

#97
TRAIT

An efficient Principal believes in teaching as a joyful experience through creative and thoughtful experiences.

➤ For him/her, teaching should be empowering self on knowledge first and then the students.

#98
TRAIT

An efficient Principal has to have empathy, integrity, responsibility and punctuality.

- It is he or she who is a benchmark for all quality attributes on campus, may these be presentation skills or communication skills or decision making in particular.

An efficient Principal has to be a bridge-builder.

- Connect people to people, people to places, people to goals and vice versa.

- Remember to narrate praises in public and criticism in private.

- Build confidence in relationships.

#100
TRAIT

An efficient Principal, as a primary leader in the school building, has to be available to teachers, staff members, parents, students and the community on a 24x7 basis.

- Must practice Kaizen as a philosophy.

During the remaining parts of the day and the night, he should learn new things and familiarize himself with those already learnt, and listen repeatedly to the things not learnt.

– Arthashastra

#101
TRAIT

An efficient Principal has to have the qualities and skills of a 'trekking guide'.

- You have to learn how to win the trust and confidence of your group the first time you meet them.

#102
TRAIT

An efficient Principal must be seen with the right people.

- Your company defines you.

- In this era of social visibility, no life is private!

- Your image strengthens your power to convince and inspire others.

#103
TRAIT

An efficient Principal must leave free and creative time at the disposal of the teachers.

- Sharing, laughing together, and sometimes not just doing anything energizes people.

- Tired teams have a low sense of belonging.

#104
TRAIT

An efficient Principal hires a great team.

- In fact, a team is better than self.

- Publishing magnate Felix Dennis used to say, "Do not seek a replica of yourself to delegate to, or to promote."

- Never duplicate your strengths and weaknesses, find people to compliment them!

SECTION 2
GET INSPIRED

Being an efficient Principal is not a job.
It's a way of life!

The next few pages host short anecdotes
to inspire the person, the teacher and the
leader in you. You must always keep the
teacher alive within the leader and vice
versa as each fires the other.

These stories are not new nor have been
written by me. They have been assorted
from various books and sources on the
internet. They have, over the years,
inspired me and have been used at various
training platforms. The takeaways are
simple but important. We know we must
do certain things in a certain way, but we
tend to forget.

They have been put together here for your
easy reading.

#1
ANECDOTE

Once a mother decided to take her young boy, who had become addicted to eating sugar, to Gandhiji for help. After a scorching tiring journey, she finally reached Gandhiji's ashram and asked him to tell her son to stop eating sugar as it wasn't good for his health.

Gandhiji refused to help at that time and asked the mother to bring the child back to him after two weeks. The mother was confused and upset and took the boy home. Two weeks later, she came back. This time Gandhiji looked directly at the boy and said, "You should stop eating sugar. It is not good for your health." The boy nodded his head and promised he wouldn't.

The boy's mother was puzzled. She asked, "Why didn't you tell him that two weeks ago when I brought him here?"

Gandhiji smiled and said, "Two weeks ago, I was eating a lot of sugar myself."

Takeaway:

Leaders must model the behaviour they ask of their subordinates.

#2
ANECDOTE

A gentleman was once walking through an elephant camp when he noticed that the elephants weren't being held by chains. All that was holding them back from escaping the camp was a small piece of rope tied to one of their legs.

The man stood there, completely confused. The elephants could easily escape from captivity using their strength to break the rope. But instead, they weren't even trying at all.

Curious and wanting to know the answer, he asked a trainer nearby why the elephants were just standing there and never tried to escape. The trainer's answer was an eye-opener. He said, "When they are very young and much smaller, we use the same size rope to tie them. At that age, it's enough to hold them. As they grow up, they are conditioned to believe they cannot break away. They believe the rope can still hold them, so they never try to break free."

The only reason that the elephants weren't breaking free was that over time they believed that it just wasn't possible.

Takeaway:

Believing you can become successful is the most important step in actually achieving it.

#3
ANECDOTE

Many years ago, in a small Italian town, a small business owner owed a large sum of money to a loan-shark. The loan-shark was a very old, unattractive man who liked the businessman's daughter. He decided to offer the businessman a deal that he would wipe out the debt if he could marry the businessman's daughter. Needless to say, this proposal was met with a look of disgust.

The loan-shark then thinking smart said that he would place two pebbles into a bag, one white and one black. The daughter would then have to reach into the bag and pick out a pebble. If it was black, he would marry the girl, and the debt would be wiped. But if it was white, the debt would be wiped, and the daughter wouldn't have to marry him.

Standing on a pebble-strewn path in the businessman's garden, the loan-shark bent over and picked up two pebbles. While he was picking them up, the daughter noticed that he'd picked up two black pebbles and placed them both into the bag.

He then asked the daughter to reach into the bag and pick one.

The daughter naturally had three choices; refuse to pick a pebble from the bag, take both pebbles out of the bag and expose the loan-shark for cheating or pick a pebble from the bag fully aware it was black and sacrifice herself for her father's freedom.

She drew out a pebble from the bag, and before looking at it, 'accidentally' dropped it into the midst of the other pebbles on the path.

She then said to the loan-shark, "Oh, how clumsy of me. Never mind, if you look into the bag for the one that is left, you will be able to tell which pebble I picked."

The pebble left in the bag was obviously black. As the loan-shark didn't want to be exposed, he had to play along with the trick and pretend as if the pebble that the daughter had dropped was white. He lost the marriage proposal and had to clear the debt as well.

Takeaway:

Smart, out-of-the-box thinking can sail you through tough situations.

#4
ANECDOTE

Four frog friends were travelling through the woods. Two of them accidentally fell into a deep pit. When the other two frogs crowded around the pit and saw how deep it was, they told the two frogs that there was no hope left for them.

However, the two frogs decided to ignore what the others said, and they attempted to jump out. This time they fell back harder and also bruised themselves. The two frogs on the top shouted harder and told them to stay safe inside, as jumping out was not possible.

Eventually, one of the frogs, believing what the others had to say, gave up. However, the other frog continued to jump as hard as he could. The three frogs now yelled at him to stop and accept his destiny to die in that pit. But he jumped even harder this time and made it out, leaving one behind in the pit.

When he got out, the other frogs said, "Did you not hear us?"

The frog explained to them that he was deaf. He thought they were encouraging him the entire time.

Takeaway:

Your thoughts are very powerful. They will make anything happen, no matter what people say.

#5
ANECDOTE

There was once a farmer who sold a pound of butter to a baker. One day the baker decided to weigh the butter to see if he was getting the right amount. When he weighed it, he found the butter of less than the ordered quantity. Angry about this, he took the farmer to court.

The judge asked the farmer if he was using any measure to weigh the butter. The farmer replied, "Sir, I am primitive. I don't have a proper measure, but I do have a scale."

The judge asked, "Then how do you weigh the butter?"

The farmer replied, "Sir, long before the baker started buying butter from me, I have been buying a pound of bread from him. Every day when the baker brings the bread, I put it on the scale and give him the same weight in butter. If anyone is to be blamed, it is the baker."

Takeaway:

In life, you get what you give. Don't try and cheat others.

#6
ANECDOTE

In ancient times, a King had a boulder placed on a roadway. He then hid and watched to see if anyone would move the boulder out of the way. Some of the King's wealthiest merchants and courtiers came by and simply walked around it.

Many people loudly blamed the King for not keeping the roads clear, but none of them did anything about getting the stone out of the way.

A peasant then came along carrying a load of vegetables. Upon approaching the boulder, the peasant laid down his burden and tried to push the stone out of the road. After much pushing and straining, he finally succeeded.

After the peasant went back to pick up his vegetables, he noticed a purse lying in the road where the boulder had been. The purse contained many gold coins and a note from the King explaining that the gold was for the person who removed the boulder from the roadway.

Takeaway:

Every obstacle we come across in life gives us an opportunity to improve our circumstances.

#7
ANECDOTE

One day a man found a cocoon of a butterfly. He noticed a small opening on one side. He sat down to watch the butterfly as it struggled to force its body through that little hole.

Suddenly it stopped making any progress and looked as if it was stuck. The man decided to help the butterfly. He took a pair of scissors and cut off the remaining bit of the cocoon. The butterfly emerged easily, although it had a swollen body and small, shrivelled wings.

The man sat there waiting for the wings to enlarge to support the butterfly to fly. But that didn't happen. The butterfly struggled there, unable to fly, crawling around with tiny wings and a swollen body to ultimately die.

The kind-hearted man didn't understand that the restricting cocoon and the struggle needed by the butterfly to

*get itself through the small opening were
God's way of forcing fluid from the body of
the butterfly into its wings, thus preparing
itself to fly to life.*

Takeaway:

*Our struggles develop our strengths.
Without them, we never grow or get
stronger.*

#8
ANECDOTE

There once was a little boy who had a very bad temper. His father decided to hand him a bag of nails and said that every time the boy lost his temper, he had to hammer a nail into the fence.

Conscious of the situation, the boy was shocked to see that he had hammered 37 nails into the fence on the first day.

The boy gradually began to control his temper over the next few weeks, and the number of nails he was hammering into the fence slowly decreased. He discovered it was easier to control his temper than to hammer those nails into the fence.

Finally, one day when the boy didn't have to hammer a single nail, he rushed to his father. The father then told the boy to pull out a nail every day he kept his temper under control.

The days passed, and the young boy was finally able to tell his father that all the nails were gone. The father took his son by the hand and led him to the fence. He said," You have done well, my son, but look at the holes in the fence. The fence will never be the same. When you say things in anger, they leave a scar just like this one."

Takeaway:

Control your anger. Don't say things to people that you may later regret.

#9
ANECDOTE

One day, an old professor was invited to lecture on 'Efficient Time Management'. Standing in front of this group of elite student-managers, who were willing to write down every word that would come out of the famous professor's mouth, he slowly met eyes with each and finally said, "We are going to conduct an experiment."

The professor pulled out a big glass jar and gently placed it in front of him on the table. Next, he pulled out a bag of stones, each the size of a tennis ball, and placed the stones one by one in the jar. He did so until there was no room for more. Lifting his gaze to the audience, the professor asked, "Is the jar full?"

They replied, "Yes."

The professor paused for a moment and then remarked, "Really?"

Once again, he reached under the table and pulled out a bag full of pebbles. Carefully, the professor poured the pebbles in and slightly rattled the jar, allowing the pebbles to slip through the larger stones until they settled at the bottom. Again, the professor asked, "Is the jar full?"

At this point, the audience began to understand his intentions. One replied, "Apparently, not!"

"Correct," replied the old professor, now pulling out a bag of sand from under the table.

Cautiously, the professor poured the sand into the jar. The sand filled up the spaces between the stones and the pebbles.

Yet again, the professor asked, "Is the jar full?"

Without hesitation, the entire group of students replied in unison, "NO!"

"Correct," replied the professor. And as was expected by the students, the professor reached for the pitcher of water and poured water in the jar until it was absolutely full. The professor now lifted his gaze once again and asked, "What great truth can we surmise from this experiment?"

With his thoughts on the lecture topic, one manager quickly replied, "We learn that as full as our schedules may appear, only if we increase our effort, it is always possible to add more meetings and tasks."

"No," replied the professor. The great truth that we can conclude from this experiment is, "If we don't put all the larger stones in the jar first, we will never be able to fit all of them later."

The auditorium fell silent, as every manager processed the significance of the professor's words in their entirety.

The old professor continued, "What are the large stones in your life? Health? Family? Friends? Your goals? Doing what you love? Fighting for a Cause? Taking time for yourself?"

What we must remember is that it is most important to include the lager stones in our lives, because if we don't do so, we are likely to miss out on life altogether. If we give priority to the smaller things in life (pebbles and sand), our lives will be filled up with less important things, leaving little or no time for the things in our lives that are most important to us.

Takeaway:

Because of this, never forget to ask yourself, "What are the Large Stones in your life?" Once you identify them, be sure to put them first in your 'Jar of Life'.

#10
ANECDOTE

It was the coldest winter ever. Many animals died because of the cold. The porcupines, realizing the situation, decided to group together to keep warm. This way, they covered and protected themselves. But the quills of each one wounded their closest companions. After a while, they decided to distance themselves. Sure enough, they began to die, alone and frozen.

So they had to make a choice—either accept the quills of their companions or disappear from the Earth. Wisely, they decided to go back to being together. They learned to live with the little wounds caused by the close relationship with their companions in order to receive the heat that came from the others. This way, they were able to survive.

The best relationship is not the one that brings together perfect people, but when each individual learns to live with the imperfections of others and can admire the other person's good qualities.

Takeaway:

Life is short, and it is up to you to make it sweet.

#11
ANECDOTE

A young man once asked Socrates about the secret to success. Socrates told the young man to meet him near the river the next morning. They met. Socrates asked the young man to walk with him towards the river. When the water got up to their neck, Socrates took the young man by surprise and ducked him into the water. The boy struggled to get out, but Socrates was strong and kept him there until the boy started turning blue.

Socrates pulled his head out of the water, and the first thing the young man did was to gasp and take a deep breath of air. Socrates asked, "What did you want the most when you were there?" The boy replied, "Air."

Socrates said, "That is the secret to success. When you want success as badly as you wanted the air, then you will get it." There is no other secret.

Takeaway:

A burning desire is the starting point of all accomplishments.

#12
ANECDOTE

Once a frog fell into a vessel full with water set on a stove to boil. Initially, the water was at a normal temperature. This did not affect the frog. Soon the temperature of the water began to rise and became warm. The frog enjoyed the warmth and continued to be there. As the temperature rose, the frog adjusted its body temperature accordingly. The frog kept adjusting its body temperature with the increasing temperature of the water.

Just when the water was about to reach the boiling point, the frog could not adjust anymore. At this point, the frog decided to jump out. The frog tried hard, but it was unable to do so because it had lost all its strength in adjusting with the rising water temperature.

Soon, the frog died.

What killed the frog? Think about it! The truth about what killed the frog is its own inability to decide when to jump out.

Takeaway:

We all need to adjust to people and situations, but we need to be sure till when we need to adjust and when we need to move on. Decide to jump while you still have the strength.

#13
ANECDOTE

During a research experiment, a marine biologist placed a shark into a large holding tank and released several small bait fish into it. As expected, the shark quickly swam around the tank, attacked and ate the smaller fish. The marine biologist then inserted a strong piece of clear fibreglass into the tank, creating two separate partitions. She then put the shark on one side of the fibreglass and a new set of bait fish on the other.

Again, the shark quickly attacked. This time, however, the shark slammed into the fibreglass divider and bounced off. Undeterred, the shark kept repeating this behaviour every few minutes but to no avail. Meanwhile, the bait fish swam around unharmed in the second partition. Eventually, about an hour into the experiment, the shark gave up.

This experiment continued over the next few weeks. Each time, the shark got less aggressive and made fewer attempts to attack the bait fish, until eventually, the shark got tired of hitting the fibreglass divider and simply stopped attacking altogether.

The marine biologist then removed the fibreglass divider, but the shark didn't attack. The shark was trained to believe a barrier existed between it and the bait fish, so the bait fish swam wherever they wished, free from harm.

Takeaway:

Similarly, many of us, after experiencing setbacks and failures, emotionally give up and stop trying. Like the shark in the story, we believe that because we were unsuccessful in the past, we will always be unsuccessful. In other words, we continue to see a barrier in our heads, even when no 'real' barrier exists between where we are and where we want to go.

NOTES

NOTES

NOTES

NOTES

REFERENCES AND MUST READS

- The 80/20 Principle: The Secret of Achieving More with Less by Richard Koch

- The Chanakya in You by Radhakrishnan Pillai

- The Winning Attitude by Jeff Keller

- How to Win Friends and Influence People by Dale Carnegie

- What Great Principals do Differently by Todd Whitaker

- The 5 Levels of Leadership by John C Maxwell

- Who Moved My Cheese? by Dr Spencer Johnson

- Learning Dispositions by Guy Claxton

- One Small Step Can Change Your Life: The Kaizen Way by Robert Maurer

Made in the USA
Las Vegas, NV
07 November 2021

33873423R00102